Look at My Tail

Written by
Cath Jones

Did you ever extend a thought about an animal's tail?

Did you ever think, "What is a tail for?"

No? You didn't?

Then let's find out about some fantastic tails.

Let's see what kinds of work they do.

I am a cat. Look at my tail!

When I swish my tail, I am saying, "Mind out!" I am reminding you that I might bite.

If I see a dog and I think it might attack me, I fluff up my tail to make myself look bigger.

I am a wood mouse. Look at my tail.

I am quite little and so is my tail. But it is long and it helps me run along things that are thin, like plants.

I am a red squirrel. Look at my tail!

My tail keeps me cool. When I get too hot, I flick up my tail to give me shade.

When I jump through the air, my tail stops me spinning around.

I am a snake. I am a **pit viper**. Look at my tail!

Yes, I do have a tail. I use it to say, "Look out! Don't mess with me!"

I can use my tail to hang from things too.

I am a pangolin. Look at my tail.

My tail is hidden behind hard scales, to defend it.

I can use my tail to hang in a tree. It helps me hold on too.

I am a humpback whale. Look at my tail!

When I slap my tail fin on the water, I am doing it to impress.

It's called **lobtailing**. SPLASH! Shall I do it again?

I am a human. I have a tail too.

Can you see it? I put it on myself. But look out, don't pull it off! My tail helps me sit upright.